Engineering Marvels

World Landmarks

Addition and Subtraction

Jennifer Prior, Ph.D.

Consultant

Lorrie McConnell, M.A.
Professional Development Specialist TK–12
Moreno Valley USD, CA

Publishing Credits

Rachelle Cracchiolo, M.S.Ed., *Publisher*
Conni Medina, M.A.Ed., *Managing Editor*
Dona Herweck Rice, *Series Developer*
Emily R. Smith, M.A.Ed., *Series Developer*
Diana Kenney, M.A.Ed., NBCT, *Content Director*
June Kikuchi, *Content Director*
Stacy Monsman, M.A., *Editor*
Michelle Jovin, M.A., *Assistant Editor*
Fabiola Sepulveda, *Graphic Designer*

Image Credits: p.12 Tommy Dixon NI Syndication/Newscom; p.14 Branimir Kvartuc/Zuma Press/Alamy; p.17 Gualtiero Boffi/Alamy; p.27 (top) Denis Charlet/AFP/Getty Images; all other images from iStock and/or Shutterstock.

Library of Congress Cataloging-in-Publication Data

Names: Prior, Jennifer Overend, 1963- author.
Title: World landmarks / Jennifer Prior.
Description: Huntington Beach, CA : Teacher Created Materials, Inc., [2018] |
  Series: Engineering marvels | Includes index. | Audience: Grades K to 3.
Identifiers: LCCN 2017055453 (print) | LCCN 2017056904 (ebook) | ISBN 9781480759992 (e-book) | ISBN 9781425857493 (pbk.)
Subjects: LCSH: Historic buildings--Juvenile literature. | Monuments--Juvenile literature. | Engineering--Juvenile literature.
Classification: LCC TA149 (ebook) | LCC TA149 .P75 2018 (print) | DDC 624--dc23
LC record available at https://lccn.loc.gov/2017055453

Teacher Created Materials
5301 Oceanus Drive
Huntington Beach, CA 92649-1030
http://www.tcmpub.com

ISBN 978-1-4258-5749-3

Table of Contents

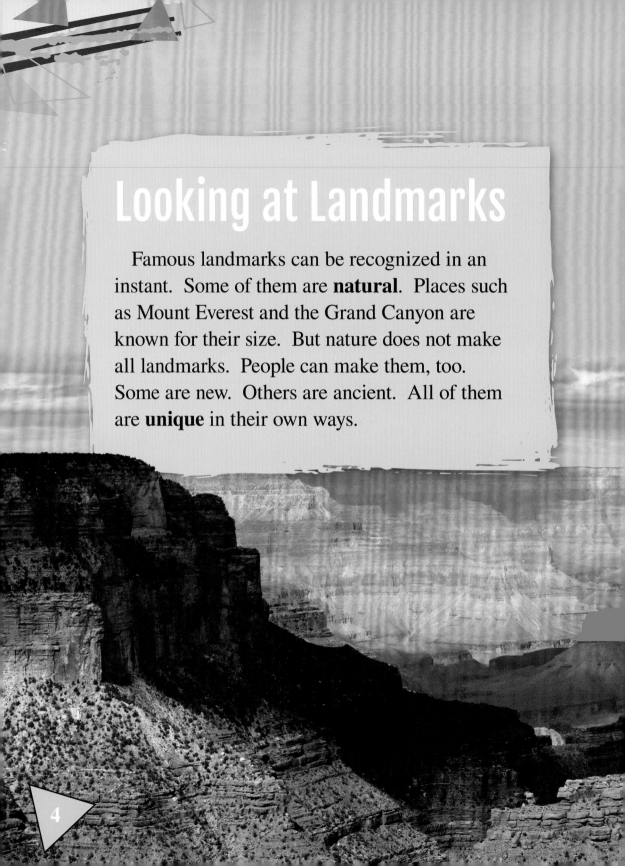

Looking at Landmarks

Famous landmarks can be recognized in an instant. Some of them are **natural**. Places such as Mount Everest and the Grand Canyon are known for their size. But nature does not make all landmarks. People can make them, too. Some are new. Others are ancient. All of them are **unique** in their own ways.

Mount Everest

Grand Canyon

North and South America

North and South America have many landmarks. Some were built in recent years. Others have been around for much longer.

Gateway Arch

St. Louis, Missouri, is called the Gateway to the West. It is home to the Gateway Arch. The **monument** was built in 1965. It **honors** all the people who **expanded** the United States by moving to the West.

The Gateway Arch is made of steel. It is 630 feet (192 meters) tall. Guests who are **brave** enough can take a tram to the top. From there, they can see for miles. It is a great place to see the sights of the city.

United States of America

Park rangers assist guests riding the tram at the Gateway Arch. Imagine that park rangers share some facts during your visit.

1. A park ranger says, "One tram can hold 240 visitors. But, it is not very crowded right now, since the tram just carried 100 fewer visitors." How many visitors were on the tram?

2. Another park ranger says, "This morning was very busy! Two trams were running. I helped 380 visitors. But the trams can hold 100 more people." How many visitors can both trams hold?

3. A third park ranger says, "Today, you can see for 20 miles at the top of the Arch. But on a clear day, it is possible to see 10 miles farther." How many miles away can you see on a clear day?

Gateway Arch

Machu Picchu

Machu Picchu (MAW-choo PEE-choo) sits high on a mountain in Peru. Hundreds of years ago, the Inka chose to live there. It was a hard place to reach. It kept them safe. Machu Picchu was hidden very well. In fact, most people did not know about it until 1911.

Today, people can see it up close. They can climb to the top, but they should prepare to sweat! They will have to climb more than three thousand steps to the top. Many people think the view is worth the climb.

Machu Picchu

There are more than 150 buildings at Machu Picchu.

Peru

LET'S EXPLORE MATH

Imagine that some tour groups are hiking Machu Picchu. There are groups of 25, 33, and 42 hikers. What math questions can you ask with this information?

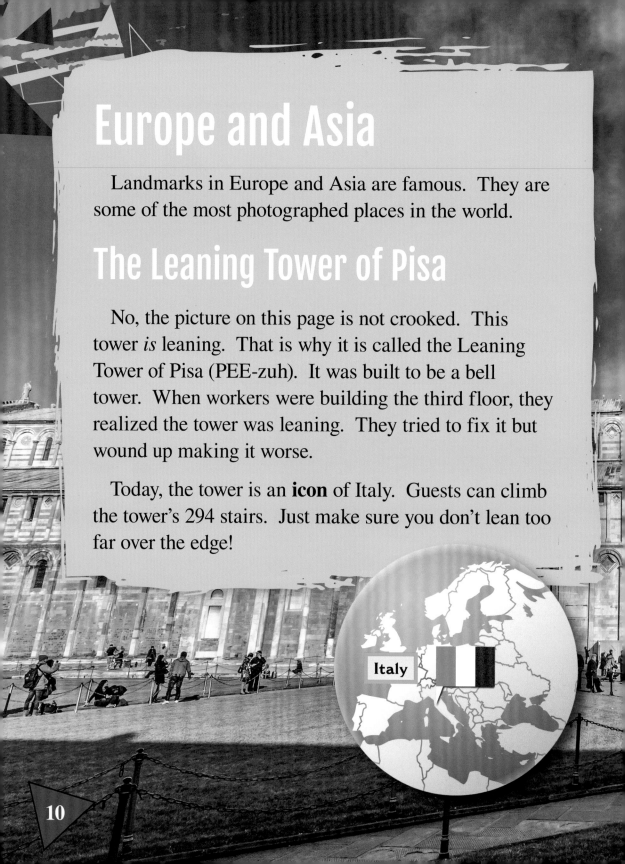

Europe and Asia

Landmarks in Europe and Asia are famous. They are some of the most photographed places in the world.

The Leaning Tower of Pisa

No, the picture on this page is not crooked. This tower *is* leaning. That is why it is called the Leaning Tower of Pisa (PEE-zuh). It was built to be a bell tower. When workers were building the third floor, they realized the tower was leaning. They tried to fix it but wound up making it worse.

Today, the tower is an **icon** of Italy. Guests can climb the tower's 294 stairs. Just make sure you don't lean too far over the edge!

Italy

The Leaning Tower of Pisa leaned the opposite way before the top four floors were built!

Big Ben

The United Kingdom is home to a tower, too. Luckily, this one does not lean. It is the Elizabeth Tower in London.

Inside the tower is a huge bell. This bell is called Big Ben. It rings at certain times of the day. Shortly after the tower was built, Big Ben cracked. The hammer that struck the bell to make it ring was too heavy. The hammer was changed for a lighter one. Today, tourists can still see the crack in the bell.

United Kingdom

A man points to Big Ben's crack in 1959.

The Elizabeth Tower (right) is part of the Palace of Westminster building. It is where members of the government work.

Saint Basil's

In Moscow, Russia, there is a famous **cathedral** called Saint Basil's. This church is more than five hundred years old. When it was built, the outside was all white. The only color came from the domes, which were gold. After about a hundred years, the church was repainted. This time, painters used bright colors on the towers.

Today, the bright building is famous. Guests love to climb the stairs to the top. From there, they have a great view of the city.

Russia

You can see other Moscow landmarks from inside Saint Basil's.

Saint Basil's Cathedral

15

Taj Mahal

A landmark in India tells a tale of love and loss. It is called the Taj Mahal (TAHJ muh-HAHL). Emperor Shah Jahān (SHAW juh-HAHN) had it built for his wife. She had died while having a baby. So, Jahān built the Taj Mahal to be her **tomb**.

Today, millions of people visit the Taj Mahal each year. For many, it is a must-see landmark.

front of the Taj Mahal

India

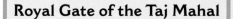

Royal Gate of the Taj Mahal

LET'S EXPLORE MATH

The main dome of the Taj Mahal is 73 meters tall. The large arch under the dome is 33 meters tall. How much taller is the main dome than the large arch? Draw a number line similar to the one below. Use it to find your solution.

⟵————————————|————⟶
                              73

Great Wall of China

The Great Wall of China is not just one wall. It is actually a chain of walls. In total, the walls are thousands of miles long.

The wall was originally built to keep people out of China. But now, the wall brings people there. In fact, more than 10 million people go to see the Great Wall each year!

This section of the Great Wall winds through one of China's mountain ranges.

China

Great Buddha

The Great Buddha statue rests in the green hills of Japan. It honors the Buddha. He was a religious figure. The huge statue is more than seven hundred years old.

When the statue was first built, it was kept in a wooden **temple**. One day, a big wave hit the temple. The temple washed away. People were shocked to see that the statue had stayed in place. It has been out in the open air ever since.

Japan

Followers of the Buddha (called Buddhists) visit the statue to pray.

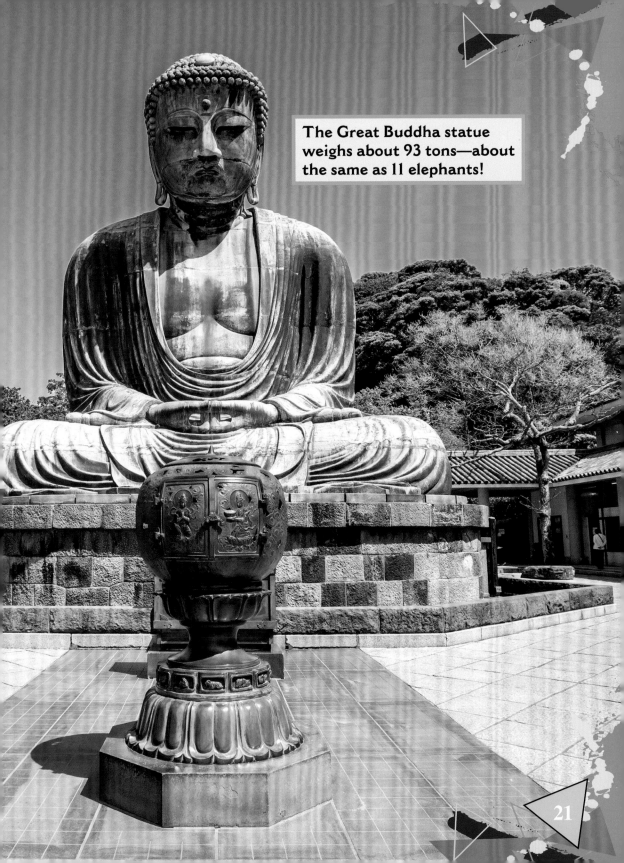

The Great Buddha statue weighs about 93 tons—about the same as 11 elephants!

Africa and Australia

The next two landmarks are thousands of miles apart. But, they are known around the world.

Pyramids of Giza

The three Pyramids of Giza are in Egypt. They are more than four thousand years old. They were used as tombs for the kings of Egypt. The oldest pyramid is the largest. It was built for King Khufu (KOO-foo). The other two were built for his son and grandson.

The middle pyramid (built for King Khufu) took about 30 years to finish.

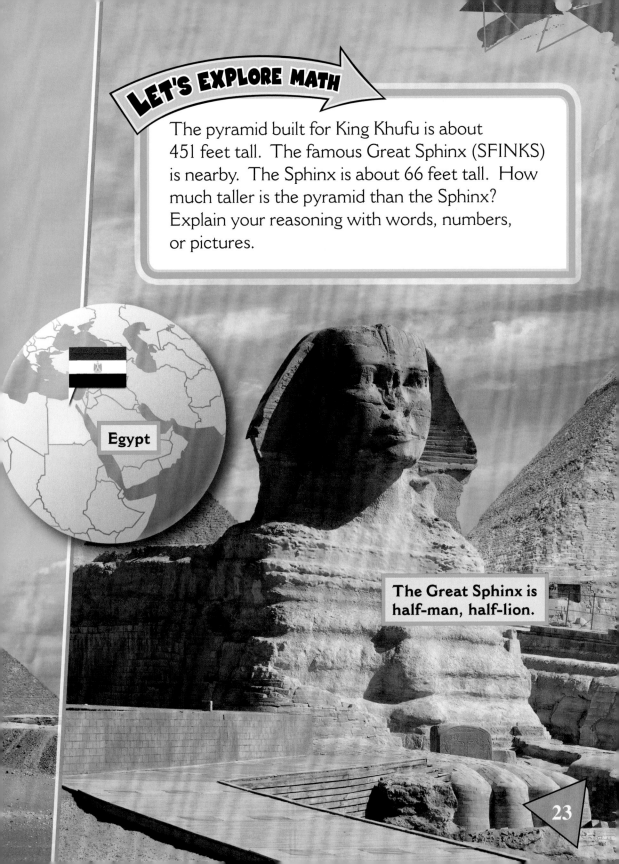

The pyramid built for King Khufu is about 451 feet tall. The famous Great Sphinx (SFINKS) is nearby. The Sphinx is about 66 feet tall. How much taller is the pyramid than the Sphinx? Explain your reasoning with words, numbers, or pictures.

Egypt

The Great Sphinx is half-man, half-lion.

Sydney Opera House

The Sydney Opera House stands near the shore in Australia. Some of the most famous singers in the world have performed there. But the true star is the building itself.

The roof has different sections. The sections are called shells. The outsides of the shells are covered in white and cream tiles. These tiles make the landmark look like it is shining!

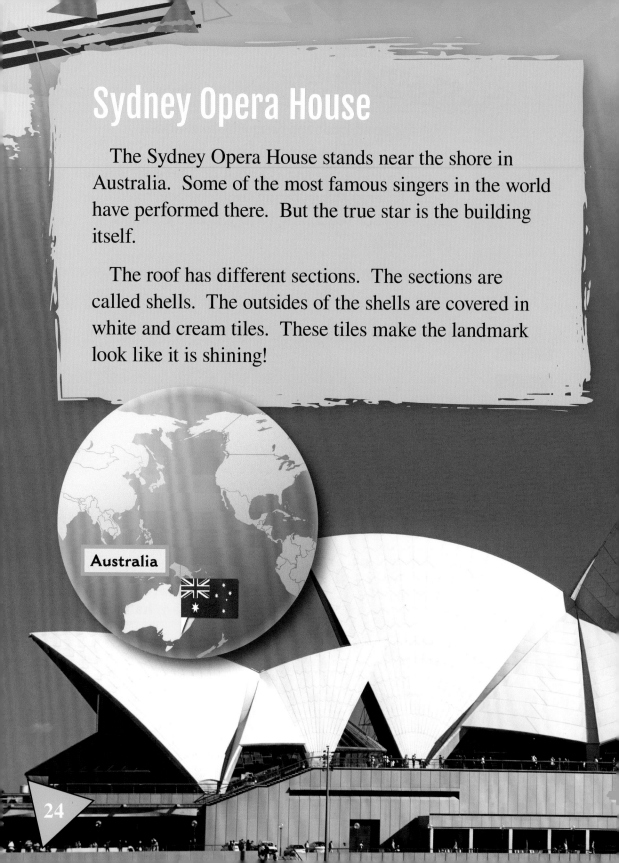

Australia

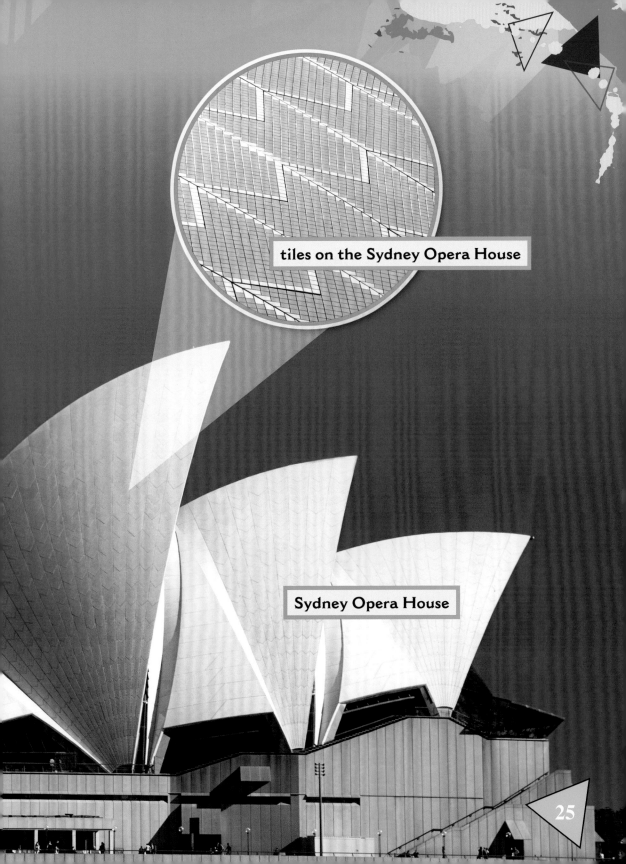

tiles on the Sydney Opera House

Sydney Opera House

Making Your Mark

What a great trip! But there are still more landmarks to discover. Mount Rushmore is massive. So is the Empire State Building. The Channel Tunnel and the Panama Canal are amazing, too. Look for landmarks. Find out what makes each one special. Who knows? Maybe you will design a landmark of your own one day!

Mount Rushmore in the United States

TUNNEL

Channel Tunnel in France

Panama Canal in Panama

⚙️ Problem Solving

The Leaning Tower of Pisa is a famous landmark in Italy. Imagine that you have been asked to design two new towers based on the original structure. Use the information to plan your towers. Then, draw diagrams to tell more about them.

1. The Leaning Tower of Pisa has 294 steps. Use this fact to plan the first tower.

   a. Use the digits 2, 9, and 4 one time each to create the greatest three-digit number possible. This will be the number of steps in your tower.

   b. Which tower has more steps: yours or the original? How many more steps does it have? Explain your reasoning with words, numbers, or pictures.

   c. How many steps do both towers have? Explain your reasoning with words, numbers, or pictures.

2. The Leaning Tower of Pisa is about 186 feet tall. Use this fact to plan the second tower.

   a. Use the digits 1, 8, and 6 one time each to create the least three-digit number possible. This will be the height of your tower.

   b. Which tower is taller: yours or the original? How much taller is it? Explain your reasoning with words, numbers, or pictures.

   c. What is the height of both towers? Explain your reasoning with words, numbers, or pictures.

Glossary

brave—having courage

cathedral—the main church of an area or region

expanded—grew

honors—shows respect for someone or something

icon—a widely known symbol or place

monument—a building, place, or statue that honors an event or person

natural—existing in nature and not caused or made by people

temple—a building that is used for religious worship

tomb—a chamber where a dead body is kept

unique—unlike anything else

Index

Answer Key

Let's Explore Math

page 7:

1. 140 visitors
2. 480 visitors
3. 30 mi.

page 9:

Answers will vary. Example: *How many total hikers are there?*, or *How many more hikers does the largest group have than the smallest group?*

page 17:

40 m taller

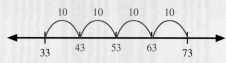

page 23:

385 ft. taller; Explanations will vary but may include equations, number lines, or skip counting.

Problem Solving

1. **a.** 942 steps

    b. Yours; 648 more steps; Explanations will vary but should show that 942 is 648 more than 294.

    c. 1,236 steps; Explanations will vary but may include equations, place value strategies, or pictures.

2. **a.** 168 ft.

    b. Original; 18 ft. taller; Explanations will vary but should show that 168 is 18 less than 186.

    c. 354 ft. tall; Explanations will vary but may include equations, pictures, or number lines.